GIFT AND MYSTERY

GIFT AND MYSTERY

On the Fiftieth Anniversary
of My Priestly Ordination

by

Pope John Paul II

IMAGE BOOKS / DOUBLEDAY

NEW YORK   LONDON   TORONTO

SYDNEY   AUCKLAND

AN IMAGE BOOK
PUBLISHED BY DOUBLEDAY
a division of Random House, Inc.
1540 Broadway, New York, New York 10036

IMAGE, DOUBLEDAY, and the portrayal of a deer drinking from
a stream are trademarks of Doubleday, a division of Random House, Inc.

Originally published in Italy as *Dono e Mistero*
by Libreria Editrice Vaticana

Gift and Mystery was published in hardcover by Doubleday in December 1996.

All biblical quotations are from the Revised Standard Version.

The English version of the Litany on page 108 is not an official translation.

Book design by Maria Carella

Library of Congress Cataloging-in-Publication Data

John Paul II, Pope, 1920–
[Dono e mistero.   English]
Gift and mystery: on the fiftieth anniversary of my priestly
ordination / by Pope John Paul II.
p.   cm.
"Image books."
1. John Paul II, Pope, 1920–   .   2. Popes—Biography.
3. Catholic Church—Poland—Clergy—Biography.   4. Priesthood.
I. Title.
BX1378.5.J5513   1999
282'.092—dc21   98-38859
[B]   CIP

ILLUSTRATIONS

1. Wadowice. Parish church of the Presentation of the Blessed Virgin Mary.
2. Wadowice. Childhood home of Pope John Paul II.
3. Cracow. *Collegium Maius* of the Jagiellonian University.
4. Cracow. Entrance of the Archbishop's Residence.
5. Kalwaria Zebrzydowska, shrine of the Blessed Virgin Mary.
6. Cracow. Steps leading to 10 Tyniecka Street.
7. Cracow. Facade of the Major Seminary.
8. Cracow. Wawel Cathedral. Altar of Saint Hedwig, Queen of Poland.
9. Cracow. Church of the Albertine Sisters. *Ecce Homo* by Brother Saint Albert.

10. Cracow. Archbishop's Residence. Altar in the Chapel.

11. Cracow. Wawel Cathedral. Crypt of Saint Leonard.

12. Niegowić. Parish church of the Assumption of the Blessed Virgin Mary.

13. Cracow. Wawel Cathedral. Confession of Saint Stanislaus, Bishop and Martyr.

14. Cracow. Parish church of Saint Florian.

15. Cracow. Wawel Cathedral.

16. Rome. Bernini colonnade and dome of Saint Peter's.

CONTENTS

I have vivid memories . . .   *1*

I

At the beginning . . . the mystery!   *3*

The first signs of my vocation   *5*

Studies at the Jagiellonian University   *6*

The outbreak of the Second World War   *8*

The theater of the living word   *10*

II

My decision to enter the seminary   *12*

Holidays as a seminarian   *16*

Cardinal Adam Stefan Sapieha   *17*

III

Influences on my vocation 19

Family 19

The Solvay plant 20

Dębniki parish: the Salesians 23

The Carmelite Fathers 24

Father Kazimierz Figlewicz 25

The "Marian thread" 27

Brother Saint Albert 31

The experience of the war 34

The sacrifices made by Polish priests 36

Goodness experienced amid the harshness of war 39

IV

A priest! 41

Remembering a brother in the priestly vocation 42

Veni, Creator Spiritus! 43

The floor 44

My first Mass 46

Among the People of God 49

V

Rome   50

"Learning Rome"   51

Pastoral perspectives   53

The European horizon   55

In the midst of immigrants   56

The figure of Saint John Mary Vianney   57

Heartfelt gratitude   58

My return to Poland   59

VI

Niegowić: a country parish   61

At Saint Florian's in Cracow   63

Scholarly work   64

VII

To the Church in Poland, thank you!   65

The presbyterate of Cracow   67

The gift of lay people   69

VIII

Who is the priest?   71

Admirabile commercium!   72

CONTENTS

The priest and the Eucharist   74

In persona Christi   76

Mysterium fidei   77

Christ, Priest and Victim   79

IX

Being a priest today   83

Humanity's profound expectations   85

A minister of mercy   86

A man in contact with God   87

Called to holiness   88

Cura animarum   89

A man of the word   91

Scholarly study   93

Dialogue with contemporary thought   94

X

To my brothers in the priesthood   96

Pupilla oculi   97

Deo gratias!   98

APPENDIX

Litany of Our Lord Jesus Christ, Priest and Victim   101

GIFT AND MYSTERY

I have vivid memories of the joyful meeting held in the Vatican last autumn (27 October 1995), under the auspices of the Congregation for the Clergy, to celebrate the thirtieth anniversary of the Second Vatican Council's Decree Presbyterorum Ordinis. *In the festive atmosphere of that gathering a number of priests spoke about their vocation, and I gave my own* testimony. *It seemed good and worthwhile that, among priests, in the presence of the people of God, this kind of mutual encouragement should be given.*

My words on that occasion received wide publicity. As a result, many people have urged me to speak more fully about my vocation during this year of my Priestly Jubilee.

I confess that at first I approached the idea with understandable hesitation. But later I felt it my duty to accept the invitation as part of the service involved in the Petrine ministry. Prompted by a series of questions asked by Mr. Gian Franco Svidercoschi, which served as an outline, I let myself be freely carried along by a wave of memories, without any intention of providing a strictly documentary account.

What I relate here, above and beyond the external events, belongs to my deepest being, to my innermost experience. I recall these things above all in order to thank the Lord. "Misericordias Domini in aeternum cantabo!" I offer this to priests and to the people of God as a testimony of love.

I

At the Beginning . . .
the Mystery!

The story of my priestly vocation? It is known above all to God. At its deepest level, every vocation to the priesthood is *a great mystery;* it is a gift which infinitely transcends the individual. Every priest experiences this clearly throughout the course of his life. Faced with the greatness of the gift, we sense our own inadequacy.

A vocation is *a mystery of divine election:* "You did not choose me, but I chose you and appointed you that you should go and bear fruit and that your fruit should abide" (Jn 15:16). "And one does not take the honor upon himself, but he is called by God, just as Aaron was" (Heb 5:4). "Before I formed you in the womb I knew you, and before you were born I consecrated you; I appointed you a prophet to the nations" (Jer 1:5). These inspired words cannot fail to move deeply the heart of every priest.

So when on certain occasions—for example at Priestly Jubilees—we speak about the priesthood and give our witness, we must do so with great humility, knowing that God "has called us with a holy calling, not in virtue of our works but in virtue of his own purpose and the grace which he gave us" (2 Tim 1:9). At the same time we realize that *human words are insufficient to do justice to the mystery* which the priesthood involves.

To me it seems essential to state this at the outset, so that what I say about my own path to the priesthood can be properly understood.

The First Signs of My Vocation

The Metropolitan Archbishop of Cracow, Prince Adam Stefan Sapieha, visited the parish of Wadowice when I was a secondary school student. My religion teacher, Father Edward Zacher, chose me to give the address of welcome. It was the first time I had the opportunity of being in the presence of that man who was so highly regarded by everyone. I know that after my speech the Archbishop asked the religion teacher what university course I would be taking upon completion of secondary school. Father Zacher replied: "He will study Polish language and letters." The Archbishop apparently replied: "A pity it is not theology."

In that period of my life *my vocation to the priesthood had not yet matured,* even though many people around me thought that I should enter the seminary. Perhaps some of them thought that if a young person with such evident religious inclinations did not enter the seminary, it had to be a sign that there were other loves or interests involved. Certainly, I knew many girls from school and, involved as I was in the school drama club, I had many opportunities to get together with other young people. But this was not the issue. At that time I was completely absorbed by a passion for *literature*, especially *dramatic literature*, and for the *theater*. I had been introduced to the theater by Mieczysław Kotlarczyk, a Polish language teacher a few years older than myself. He was a true pioneer of amateur theater and had great ambitions of building a serious repertoire.

Studies at
the Jagiellonian University

In May 1938 I passed the secondary school examination and entered the University to study Polish language and letters. My father and I moved from Wadowice to Cracow and set up house at 10 Tyniecka Street, in the Dębniki district. The house belonged to relatives of my mother. I began my studies in the *Faculty of Philosophy at the Jagiellonian University*, taking courses in Polish language and letters, but I was able to complete only the first year, since the Second World War broke out on 1 September 1939.

As for my studies, I would like to point out that my choice of Polish language and letters was determined by a clear inclination towards literature. Right from the beginning of the first year, however, I found myself attracted to *the study of the language itself*. We studied the descriptive grammar of modern Polish as well as the historical evolution of the language, with a special interest in its ancient Slavic roots. This opened up completely new horizons for me; it introduced me to *the mystery of language itself*.

The word, before it is ever spoken on the stage, is already present in human history as a fundamental dimension of man's spiritual experience. Ultimately, the mystery of language brings us back to *the inscrutable mystery of God himself.* As I came to appreciate the power of the word in my literary and linguistic studies, I inevitably drew closer to the mystery of the Word—that Word of which we speak every day in the *Angelus:* "And the Word became flesh and dwelt among us" (Jn 1:14). Later I came to realize that my study of Polish language and letters had prepared the ground for a different kind of interest and study. It had prepared me for an encounter with philosophy and theology.

The Outbreak of the Second World War

But let us go back to 1 September 1939. The outbreak of the war radically changed the course of my life. True, the professors of the Jagiellonian University tried to start the new academic year in the usual way, but lectures lasted only until 6 November 1939. On that day the German authorities assembled all the teachers in a meeting which ended with the deportation of those distinguished scholars to the Sachsenhausen concentration camp. The period of my life devoted to the study of Polish language and letters thus came to an end, and *the period of the German occupation began.* During that time I tried at first to do a lot of reading and writing. My first literary works date back to that period.

In order to avoid deportation to do forced labor in

Germany, I began in the autumn of 1940 to work as a laborer in a stone quarry attached to the Solvay chemical plant. This was at Zakrzówek, about half an hour from my home in Dębniki, and every day I would walk there. I later wrote a poem about that quarry. Rereading it after so many years, I still find that it expresses very well that extraordinary experience:

> Listen: the even knocking of hammers,
> so much their own,
> I project on to the people
> to test the strength of each blow.
> Listen now, electric current
> cuts through a river of rock.
> And a thought grows in me day after day:
> the greatness of work is inside man.
>
> *(The Quarry, I, Material, 1)*

I was present when, during the detonation of a dynamite charge, some rocks struck a worker and killed him. The experience left a profound impression on me:

They took his body, and walked in a silent line.
Toil still lingered about him, a sense of wrong.

*(The Quarry, IV, In memory
of a fellow worker, 2–3)*

The managers of the quarry, who were Poles, tried to spare us students from the heaviest work. In my case, they made me the assistant to the rock-blaster: his name was Franciszek Łabuś. I remember him because he would occasionally say things like: "Karol, you should be a priest. You have a good voice and will sing well; then you'll be all set. . . ." He said this in all simplicity, expressing a view then widely held in society about how priests lived. These words of the old workman have stuck in my memory.

The Theater of the Living Word

During that time I stayed in contact with the *theater of the living word* which Mieczysław Kotlarczyk had founded and continued to direct in the underground. At the beginning my involvement in the theater was helped by having Kotlarczyk and his wife Sofia as guests in my home; they had managed to move from Wadowice to Cracow, within the Governorate General territory. We all lived in the same house. I was working as a laborer, he as a tram-driver at first, and later as an office-worker. Sharing the same house, we were able not only to continue our conversations about the theater, but also to attempt some actual performances. These took the form, precisely, of a theater of the word. It was all quite simple. The scenery and decoration were kept to a minimum; our efforts were concentrated essentially on the delivery of the poetic text.

The recitations took place before a small group of people whom we knew, and before guests who, because they had a particular interest in literature, belonged in a sense to the "initiated." It was essential to keep these theatrical get-togethers secret; otherwise we risked serious punishment from the occupying forces, even deportation to the concentration camps. I must admit that that whole experience of the theater left a deep impression on me, even though at a certain point I came to realize that *this was not my real vocation.*

II

*My Decision
to Enter the Seminary*

In the autumn of 1942 I made *my final decision* to enter the Cracow seminary, which was operating clandestinely. I was accepted by the Rector, Father Jan Piwowarczyk. The matter had to be kept strictly secret, even from those dear to me. I began my studies at the Theology Faculty of the Jagiellonian University, which was also clandestine, while I continued to work as a laborer at Solvay.

During the time of the occupation the Metropolitan Archbishop set up the seminary, clandestinely, at his residence. This could have led at any moment to severe repression directed against the superiors and the seminarians by the German authorities. I took up my lodging in this unusual seminary, with the much-loved Prince Metropolitan, in September 1944 and was able to stay there with my fellow students until 18 January 1945, the day—or rather the night—of the liberation. It was in fact at night that the Red Army reached the outskirts of Cracow. The retreating Germans blew up Dębniki Bridge. I remember that terrible explosion: the blast broke all the windows of the Archbishop's residence. At that moment we were in the chapel for a ceremony with the Archbishop. The following day we worked quickly to repair the damage.

But I must return to the long months which preceded the liberation. As I have said, I lived with the other young men in the Archbishop's residence. From the very beginning he had introduced us to a young priest who was to be our spiritual director. This was Father Stanisław Smoleński, a man of deep spirituality who had received his doctorate in Rome: today he is retired Auxiliary Bishop of Cracow. Father Smoleński took on the task of systematically preparing us for the priesthood. Previously our only superior had been a prefect: Father Kazimierz Kłósak. He had studied at Louvain and was a professor of philosophy; we respected and admired him greatly for his asceticism and kindness. He was immediately responsible to the Archbishop, on whom our own underground seminary also directly depended. After the summer holidays of 1945, Father Karol Kozłowski, who was from Wadowice and who had been spiritual director of the seminary before the war, was called to replace Father Jan Piwowarczyk as rector of the seminary in which he had spent almost his whole life.

Thus the years of my seminary formation went by. The first two years, those devoted to the study of philosophy, I completed clandestinely, while working as a laborer. The next two, 1944 and 1945, saw me become increasingly involved at the Jagiellonian University, even though the program of studies was very incomplete that first year following the war. The 1945–1946 academic year, however, was normal. In the Theology Faculty I had the good fortune of having a number of outstanding professors, like Father

Władysław Wicher, professor of moral theology, and Father Ignacy Różycki, professor of dogmatic theology, who introduced me to scientific methodology in theology. Today I think back with deep gratitude to all the superiors, spiritual directors, and professors who contributed to my formation during my time at the seminary. May the Lord repay their efforts and sacrifice!

At the beginning of my fifth year the Archbishop decided that I should go to Rome to finish my studies. And so, a little earlier than my companions, *I was ordained a priest on 1 November 1946.* That year our group was of course not very large: we were seven in all. Today only three of us are still alive. Our being few in number had its advantages: it enabled us to know one another very well and form bonds of friendship. This was also true, in a way, of our relationships with the superiors and professors, both in the clandestine period and in the brief period of official studies at the University.

Holidays as a Seminarian

From the beginning of my time in the seminary I began to spend my holidays in a new way. I was sent by the Archbishop *to the parish of Raciborowice,* on the outskirts of Cracow. I must express my profound gratitude to the parish priest, Father Józef Jamróz, and the curates of that parish, who became life-long friends to a young clandestine seminarian. I especially remember Father Franciszek Szymonek, who later, during the Stalinist terror, was arraigned and put on trial in order to intimidate the Church authorities in Cracow: he was condemned to death. Fortunately, after a brief period he was granted a reprieve. I also recall Father Adam Biela, who had been a few years ahead of me in secondary school in Wadowice. Thanks to these young priests, I became familiar with the Christian life of the whole parish.

Soon afterwards, a large district called Nowa Huta was built in the area around the village of Bieńczyce, which was part of the parish of Raciborowice. I spent many days there during my holidays in 1944 and also in 1945, after the war had ended. I used to make long visits to the old church in Raciborowice, which dated back to the time of Jan Długosz. There I spent many hours in meditation, walking in the cemetery. I had brought to Raciborowice the books I needed for my studies: volumes of Saint Thomas with commentaries. I was learning my theology, so to speak, from the "center" of a great theological tradition. At that time I also began to write a work on Saint John of the Cross, which I then continued under the direction of Father Ignacy Różycki, a lecturer at the University of Cracow, when the University was reopened. I later completed this work at the *Angelicum*, under the direction of Father Garrigou Lagrange.

Cardinal Adam Stefan Sapieha

A powerful influence on our whole period of formation for the priesthood was exercised by *the towering figure of the Prince Metropolitan,* the future Cardinal Adam Stefan Sapieha, whom I remember with affection and gratitude. His influence on us was increased by the fact that, during the period of transition before the reopening of the seminary, we lived in his residence and met him every day. The Metropolitan of Cracow was made a cardinal immediately after the end of the war, when he was quite old. All the people welcomed this appointment as a worthy acknowledgment of the merits of a great man who throughout the German occupation had succeeded in holding high the honor of the nation, clearly displaying his own dignity before all.

I remember that March day—it was in Lent—when the Archbishop returned from Rome after receiving his cardinal's hat. The students physically lifted up his car and carried it some distance, as far as the Basilica of the Assumption in Market Square. This was their way of expressing the religious and patriotic enthusiasm which his appointment as cardinal had inspired in the people.

III

Influences on My Vocation

I have spoken at length about my seminary experience because this was certainly the greatest influence on my priestly formation. But looking at the fuller picture, I clearly see that a number of other situations and individuals had a positive influence on me, and that God was using them to make his voice heard.

Family

My preparation for the priesthood in the seminary was *in a certain sense* preceded by the preparation I received *in my family,* thanks to the life and example of my parents. Above all I am grateful to *my father,* who became a widower at an early age. I had not yet made my First Holy Communion when I lost my mother: I was barely nine years old. So I do not have a clear awareness of her contribution, which must have been great, to my religious training. After her death and, later, the death of my older brother, I was left alone with my father, a deeply religious man. Day after day I was able to observe the austere way in which he lived. By profession he was a soldier and, after my mother's death, his life became one of constant prayer. Sometimes I would wake up during the night and find my father on his knees, just as I would always see him kneeling in the parish church. We never spoke about a vocation to the priesthood, but *his example was in a way my first seminary,* a kind of domestic seminary.

The Solvay Plant

Later, after my early years, *the stone quarry and water purification facility* in the bicarbonate plant at Borek

Fałęcki became my seminary; this was not a mere *pre-seminary* as at Wadowice. For me, at that point in my life, the plant was a true seminary, albeit a secret one. I began to work in the stone quarry in September 1940; a year later I passed to the plant's water purification facility. Those were the years when my final decision matured. In the autumn of 1942 I began my studies in the underground seminary as a former student of Polish language and letters, while still a worker at Solvay. At the time I did not realize how important that experience would be for me. Only later, as a priest, during my studies in Rome, when my colleagues at the Belgian College made me aware of the issue of worker-priests and the Young Christian Worker movement (JOC), did I realize how important contact with the world of work had become for the Church and the priesthood in the West. This contact was already a part of my life experience.

In fact, my experience had not been that of a "worker-priest" but of a "worker-seminarian." Having worked with my hands, I knew quite well the meaning of physical labor. Every day I had been with people who did heavy work. I came to know their living situations, their families, their interests, their human worth, and their dignity. I personally experienced many kindnesses from them. They knew that I was a student and they knew that, when circumstances permitted, I would return to my studies. I never encountered hostility on this account. It did not bother them that I brought books to work. They would say: "We'll keep watch: you go ahead and read." This happened especially during the night shifts. They would often say: "You go and take a break, we'll keep an eye open."

I made friends with the workers. Sometimes they invited me to their homes. Later, as a priest and Bishop, I baptized their children and grandchildren, blessed their marriages, and officiated at many of their funerals. I was also able to observe their deep but quiet religiosity and their great wisdom about life. These contacts, as I have said, remained very close, even after the German occupation ended, virtually up to the day of my election as Bishop of Rome. Some of them are still maintained through correspondence.

Dębniki Parish: the Salesians

I must take another step backwards, to the time before I entered the seminary. I cannot fail to mention
one particular place and, within it, a person from
whom I really received much during that period. The
place was *my parish,* dedicated to Saint Stanislaus
Kostka, at Dębniki in Cracow. The parish was run by
the Salesian Fathers, who one day were deported by
the Nazis to a concentration camp. Only an old parish priest and the provincial inspector remained; all
the others were interned at Dachau. I believe that *the
presence of the Salesians* played an important role in the
formation of my vocation.

In the parish there was one person who stood out
from the others: I am speaking of *Jan Tyranowski.* By
profession he was a clerk, although he had chosen to
work in his father's tailor shop. He said that working
as a tailor made it easier for him to develop his
interior life. He was a man of especially deep spirituality. The Salesian Fathers, who had courageously begun anew their work among youth in that difficult
period, had given him the task of creating a network

of contacts with young people through what was called the "Living Rosary." In carrying out this work, Jan Tyranowski did not limit himself to the organizational aspects alone; he also concerned himself with the spiritual formation of the young people whom he met. Thus I learned the basic methods of self-formation which would later be confirmed and developed in the seminary program. Tyranowski, whose own spiritual formation was based on the writings of Saint John of the Cross and Saint Teresa of Ávila, helped me to read their works, something uncommon for a person my age.

The Carmelite Fathers

This increased my interest in Carmelite spirituality. In Cracow, on Rakowicka Street, there was a monastery of *Discalced Carmelite Fathers.* I spent time with them and once made my retreat with them, under the direction of Father Leonard of Our Lady of Sorrows.

For a time I also considered entering the Carmel. My uncertainties were resolved by the Archbishop,

Cardinal Sapieha, who in his typical manner said tersely: "First you have to finish what you have begun." And that is what happened.

Father Kazimierz Figlewicz

In those years, *my confessor and spiritual director* was Father Kazimierz Figlewicz. I had first met him while I was in my first year of secondary school in Wadowice. Father Figlewicz, who was curate of the parish of Wadowice, taught us religion. Thanks to him I grew closer to the parish, became an altar server, and had a hand in organizing the group of altar servers. When he left Wadowice to go to the Cathedral of Cracow, located in the old Royal Castle of Wawel, I remained in contact with him. I remember that during my fifth year of secondary school he invited me to Cracow to take part in the Sacred Triduum, beginning with the *Tenebrae* service on the afternoon of Wednesday of Holy Week. The experience made a profound impression on me.

After graduation, when my father and I moved to

Cracow, I grew closer to Father Figlewicz; he was curate at the Cathedral. I would go to him for confession and often visited him during the German occupation.

I will never forget the day of 1 September 1939: it was the First Friday of the month. I had gone to Wawel for confession; the Cathedral was completely empty. That was perhaps the last time that I was able to enter the church freely. It was later closed and the Royal Castle of Wawel became the headquarters of the Nazi Governor-General, Hans Frank. Father Figlewicz was the only priest allowed to celebrate Mass, twice a week, in the closed Cathedral and under the vigilance of German policemen. In those difficult times it became even clearer what all this meant for him—the Cathedral, the royal tombs, the altar of Saint Stanislaus, Bishop and Martyr. Until his death, Father Figlewicz remained the faithful guardian of that special shrine of the Church and of the nation; he instilled in me a great love for the Cathedral at Wawel, which would one day be my episcopal Cathedral.

On 1 November 1946 I was ordained a priest.

The following day, for my first Mass, celebrated at the Cathedral in the crypt of Saint Leonard, Father Figlewicz stood beside me and acted as my guide. This dedicated priest has now been dead some years. Only the Lord can repay him for all the good he did for me.

The "Marian Thread"

Naturally, in speaking of the origins of my priestly vocation, *I cannot overlook its Marian thread.* I learned the traditional devotions to the Mother of God in my family and in my parish at Wadowice. I remember, in the parish church, a side chapel dedicated to Our Lady of Perpetual Help. In the mornings, the secondary school students would make a visit to it before classes began. After classes, in the afternoon, many students would go there to pray to the Blessed Virgin.

Also, on a hilltop in Wadowice, there was a Carmelite monastery which dated back to the time of Saint Raphael Kalinowski. People from Wadowice

would go there in great numbers, and this was reflected in the widespread *use of the scapular of Our Lady
of Mount Carmel.* I too received the scapular, I think at
the age of ten, and I still wear it. People also went to
the Carmelites for confession. And so, both in the
parish church and in the Carmelite monastery church,
my devotion to Mary took shape from the years of
my early childhood and adolescence up through secondary school.

When I was in Cracow, in Dębniki, I joined the
"Living Rosary" group in the Salesian parish. There
was a special devotion there to Mary, Help of Chris-
tians. In Dębniki, at the time when my priestly vocation was developing, under the influence, as I mentioned, of Jan Tyranowski, a change took place in my
understanding of devotion to the Mother of God. I
was already convinced that *Mary leads us to Christ,* but
at that time I began to realize also that *Christ leads us
to his Mother.* At one point I began to question my
devotion to Mary, believing that, if it became too
great, it might end up compromising the supremacy
of the worship owed to Christ. At that time, I was
greatly helped by a book by Saint Louis Marie Grig-

nion de Montfort entitled *Treatise of True Devotion to the Blessed Virgin.* There I found the answers to my questions. Yes, Mary does bring us closer to Christ; she does lead us to him, provided that we live her mystery in Christ. This treatise by Saint Louis Marie Grignion de Montfort can be a bit disconcerting, given its rather florid and baroque style, but the essential theological truths which it contains are undeniable. The author was an outstanding theologian. His Mariological thought is rooted in the mystery of the Trinity and in the truth of the Incarnation of the Word of God.

I then came to understand why the Church says the *Angelus* three times a day. I realized how important are the words of that prayer: "The Angel of the Lord declared unto Mary and she conceived of the Holy Spirit. . . . Behold the handmaid of the Lord: be it done unto me according to your word. . . . And the Word became flesh and dwelt among us. . . ." Such powerful words! They express the deepest reality of the greatest event ever to take place in human history.

This is the origin of the motto *Totus Tuus.* The

phrase comes from Saint Louis Marie Grignion de Montfort. It is an abbreviation of a more complete form of entrustment to the Mother of God which runs like this: *Totus Tuus ego sum et omnia mea Tua sunt. Accipio Te in mea omnia. Praebe mihi cor Tuum, Maria.*

And so, thanks to Saint Louis, I began to discover the immense riches of Marian devotion from new perspectives. As a child, for example, I would listen to the singing of the "Hours of the Immaculate Conception of the Blessed Virgin Mary" in the parish church, but only afterwards did I realize their rich theological and biblical content. So too with popular folksongs, such as the Polish Christmas carols and the Lenten Lamentations on the Passion of Jesus Christ, which highlight the soul's dialogue with the Sorrowful Mother.

These spiritual experiences were fundamental in shaping *that journey of prayer and contemplation* which gradually brought me to the priesthood, and which would later continue to guide me in all the events of my life. Even as a child, and still more as a priest and Bishop, it would lead me to make frequent Marian pilgrimages to Kalwaria Zebrzydowska. Kalwaria is the principal Marian shrine of the Archdiocese of Cracow. I would go there often, walking along its paths in solitude and presenting to the Lord in prayer the various problems of the Church, especially in the difficult times during the struggle against communism. As I look back, I see how all things are connected: today as yesterday, *we find ourselves no less deeply caught up in the same mystery.*

Brother Saint Albert

I sometimes wonder what role was played in my vocation by *Brother Saint Albert.* Adam Chmielowski—this was his name—was not a priest. Everyone in Poland knows who he was. In the period of my enthusiasm for rhapsodic theater and for art, I was deeply inspired by the figure of this courageous man, who had taken part in the "January Uprising" of 1864 and lost a leg in the fighting. Brother Albert was a painter who had studied in Munich. The artistic works which he left behind show that he had great talent. And yet, at a certain point in his life, this man abandoned his artistic pursuits because he realized that God was calling him to much more important tasks. Once he became aware of the distressing situation of Cracow's poor, who would gather in the public dormitory known as the "warming-up place" on Krakowska Street, Adam Chmielowski decided to become one of them, not as an almsgiver coming from outside to distribute gifts, but as one completely devoted to the service of the underprivileged.

This inspiring example of sacrifice attracted many followers. Men and women gathered around Brother Albert. Two religious congregations devoted to the poorest of the poor were born. All of this took place at the beginning of our own century, just before the First World War.

Brother Saint Albert would not live to see the day that Poland regained its independence. He died on Christmas Day 1916. His work, however, would continue after his death, becoming an expression of the Polish traditions of radical Gospel idealism, in the footsteps of Saint Francis of Assisi and Saint John of the Cross.

Brother Albert has a special place in the history of Polish spirituality. For me he was particularly important, because I found in him a real *spiritual support and example* in leaving behind the world of art, literature and the theater, and *in making the radical choice of a vocation to the priesthood.* One of my greatest joys as Pope was to raise this poor man of Cracow, who went about in his gray habit, to the honors of the altar, first with his beatification in Błonie Krakowskie during my visit to Poland in 1983, and then with his canonization in Rome, in November of the memorable year 1989. Many writers have immortalized the figure of Brother Albert in Polish literature. Worthy of mention among these various artistic works, novels, and plays is the monograph dedicated to him by Father Konstanty Michalski. I too, as a young priest, when I was curate at Saint Florian's Church in Cracow, wrote a dramatic work in his honor, entitled *The Brother of Our God.* This was my way of repaying a debt of gratitude to him.

The Experience of the War

As I have already said, my priestly vocation took definitive shape at the *time of the Second World War,* during the Nazi occupation. Was this a mere coincidence or was there a more profound connection between what was developing within me and external historical events? It is hard to answer such a question. Certainly, in God's plan nothing happens by chance. All I can say is that the tragedy of the war had its effect on my gradual choice of a vocation. It helped me to understand in a new way *the value and importance of a vocation.* In the face of the spread of evil and the atrocities of the war, the meaning of the priesthood and its mission in the world became much clearer to me.

The outbreak of the war took me away from my studies and from the University. In that period I also lost my father, the last remaining member of my immediate family. All this brought with it, objectively, *a progressive detachment* from my earlier plans; in a way it was like being uprooted from the soil in which, up till that moment, my humanity had grown.

But the process was not merely negative. At the same time a light was beginning to shine ever more brightly in the back of my mind: *the Lord wants me to become a priest.* One day I saw this with great clarity: it was like an interior illumination which brought with it the joy and certainty of a new vocation. And this awareness filled me with great inner peace.

All this happened against the backdrop of the terrible events taking place all around me in Cracow, Poland, Europe, and the world. I experienced directly only a small part of what my fellow countrymen experienced from 1939 onwards. I think especially of my classmates in Wadowice, close friends, some of whom were Jews. A few had already enrolled for military service in 1938. I believe that the first to die in the war was the youngest member of our class. Later I came to learn in the most general terms about the fate of others who fell on the various fronts, or died in concentration camps, or fought at Tobruk and Montecassino, or were deported to the territories of the Soviet Union: Russia and Kazakhstan. At first I learned of these things only gradually, then more completely at Wadowice in 1948, at a gathering of former classmates on the tenth anniversary of our graduation.

I was spared much of the immense and horrible drama of the Second World War. I could have been arrested any day, at home, in the stone quarry, in the plant, and taken away to a concentration camp. Sometimes I would ask myself: so many young people of my own age are losing their lives, *why not me?* Today I know that it was not mere chance. Amid the overwhelming evil of the war, everything in my own personal life was tending towards the good of my vocation. I cannot forget the kindnesses shown to me in that difficult period by people whom the Lord placed on my path, both the members of my family and my colleagues and friends.

The Sacrifices
Made by Polish Priests

This brings up another special and significant aspect of my vocation. The years of German occupation in the West and Soviet occupation in the East brought about the *arrest and deportation to concentration camps of an immense number of Polish priests.* In Dachau alone about three thousand were interned. There were other camps, like Auschwitz, where Saint Maximilian Maria Kolbe, the Franciscan of Niepokalanów, gave his life for Christ; he became the first priest to be canonized after the war. Among the prisoners at Dachau was Bishop Michał Kozal of Włocławek, whom I had the joy of beatifying in Warsaw in 1987. After the war some of the priests who had been interned in the concentration camps were elevated to the episcopate. Archbishops Kazimierz Majdański and Adam Kozłowiecki and Bishop Ignacy Jeż are still living today; as the last three Bishops who witnessed what went on in the extermination camp of Dachau, they know very well what that experience meant for the lives of so many priests. To complete the picture, I must also mention the German priests of the same period who shared the same fate in the concentration camps. I have had the honor of beatifying several of them: first, Father Rupert Mayer of Munich and then, during my most recent Apostolic Journey to Germany, Monsignor Bernhard Lichtenberg, parish priest of the Berlin Cathedral, and Father Karl Leisner of the Diocese of Münster. Father Leisner, ordained priest in the concentration camp in 1944, was able to celebrate Holy Mass only once after his ordination.

A special mention must also be made of *the martyrology of priests interned in the camps of Siberia and in other camps in the territory of the Soviet Union.* Among the many who were imprisoned there I would like to mention Father Tadeusz Fedorowicz, a well-known figure in Poland, to whom I am personally much indebted for his spiritual direction. Father Fedorowicz, a young priest of the Archdiocese of Lwow, had of his own free will gone to his Archbishop to ask if he could accompany a group of Poles being deported to the East. Archbishop Twardowski gave his permission and so Father Fedorowicz was able to carry out his priestly mission among his fellow countrymen dispersed throughout the territories of the Soviet Union, Kazakhstan in particular. He has recently described these tragic events in a fascinating book.

Of course, what I have said about the concentration camps represents only a part, albeit dramatic, of this "apocalypse" of our century. I have brought it up in order to emphasize that *my priesthood, even at its beginning, was in some way marked by the great sacrifice of countless men and women of my generation.* Providence spared me the most difficult experiences; and so my sense of indebtedness is all the greater, both to people whom I knew and to many more whom I did not know; all of them, regardless of nationality or language, by their sacrifice on the great altar of history, helped to make my priestly vocation a reality. In a way these people guided me to this path; by their sacrifice they showed me the most profound and essential truth about the priesthood of Christ.

Goodness Experienced
Amid the Harshness of War

I have said that during the difficult years of the war I experienced many kindnesses from people. I am thinking especially *of one family, indeed of many families, whom I knew during the occupation.* I had worked with Juliusz Kydryński, first in the stone quarries and then in the Solvay plant. We were in the group of student-workers which also included Wojciech Żukrowski, Wojciech's younger brother Antoni, and Wiesław Kaczmarczyk. Juliusz Kydryński and I had known each other before the war, having been together in the first year of Polish language and letters. During the war our friendship grew. I knew his mother, who was a widow, his sister, and his younger brother. The Kydryński family showed me much kindness, affection, and concern when, on 18 February 1941, I lost my father. I remember that day so very clearly: I returned home from work and found my father dead. My friendship with the Kydryńskis was a great comfort for me at the time. Our friendship then grew to include other families, especially the Szkocki family, who lived on Księcia Józefa Street. I began to study French thanks to Mrs. Jadwiga Lewaj, who lived in their house. The Szkockis' eldest daughter, Zofia Poźniak, whose husband was in a prison camp, would invite us to concerts in her home. In this way the dark period of the war and the occupation was brightened by the light of the beauty which radiates from music and poetry. All of this took place before I decided to enter the seminary.

IV

A Priest!

My ordination took place on an unusual day for such celebrations: it was on 1 November, the Solemnity of All Saints, when the Church's liturgy is wholly directed to celebrating the mystery of the Communion of Saints and preparing to commemorate the faithful departed. The Archbishop had chosen that date because I was scheduled to leave for Rome to continue my studies. I was ordained by myself, in the private chapel of the Archbishops of Cracow. My classmates were to be ordained the following year, on Palm Sunday.

I had been ordained subdeacon and deacon in

October. It was a month of intense prayer, punctuated by spiritual exercises aimed at preparing me to receive Holy Orders: six days of retreat before subdiaconate, and then three and six days respectively before diaconate and priesthood. I made the final retreat by myself in the seminary chapel. The morning of All Saints Day I presented myself at the residence of the Archbishops of Cracow, 3 Franciszkańska Street, to be ordained a priest. A small group of relatives and friends was present at the ceremony.

Remembering a Brother
in the Priestly Vocation

My ordination took place, as I said, in *the private chapel of the Archbishops of Cracow.* I remember that during the occupation I would often go there in the morning, to serve Mass for the Prince Metropolitan. I also remember that for a time another clandestine seminarian, Jerzy Zachuta, would come with me. One day he did not appear. After Mass I stopped by his house in Ludwinów (near Dębniki) and learned that he had been taken away by the Gestapo during the night. Immediately afterwards, his name appeared on the list of Poles who were to be shot. Being ordained in that very chapel which had seen us together so many times, I could not help but remember this brother in the priestly vocation, whom Christ had united in a different way to the mystery of his Death and Resurrection.

Veni, Creator Spiritus!

I can still remember myself in that chapel during the singing of the *Veni, Creator Spiritus* and the Litany of the Saints, lying prostrate on the floor with arms outstretched in the form of a cross, awaiting the moment of the imposition of hands. It was a very moving experience! Subsequently I have presided many times over this same rite as a Bishop and as Pope. There is something very impressive about the prostration of the ordinands, symbolizing as it does their total submission before the majesty of God and their complete openness to the action of the Holy Spirit who will descend upon them and consecrate them. *Veni, Creator Spiritus, mentes Tuorum visita, imple superna gratia quae Tu creasti pectora.* Just as in the Mass the Holy Spirit brings about the transubstantiation of the bread and wine into the Body and Blood of Christ, so also in the Sacrament of Holy Orders he effects the priestly or episcopal consecration. The Bishop who confers the Sacrament of Holy Orders is the human dispenser of this divine mystery. The imposition of hands is the continuation of the gesture used by the early Church to signify that the Holy Spirit is being given for a specific mission (cf. Acts 6:6, 8:17, 13:3). Paul imposed hands on the disciple Timothy (cf. 2 Tim 1:6; 1 Tim 4:14), and the gesture has remained in the Church (cf. 1 Tim 5:22) as the efficacious sign of the Holy Spirit's active presence in the Sacrament of Holy Orders.

The Floor

The one about to receive Holy Orders prostrates himself completely and rests his forehead on the church floor, indicating in this way his *complete willingness to undertake the ministry* being entrusted to him. That rite has deeply marked my priestly life. Years later, in Saint Peter's Basilica (this was at the very beginning of the Council), I was thinking back on that moment of ordination to priesthood and I wrote a poem. I would like to share a few lines of that poem here:

> Peter, you are the floor, that others
> may walk over you . . . not knowing
> where they go. You guide their steps
> . . .
> You want to serve their feet that pass
> as rock serves the hooves of sheep.
> The rock is a gigantic temple floor,
> the cross a pasture.
>
> *(The Church: Shepherds and Springs,*
> Saint Peter's Basilica, Autumn 1962,
> 11 October–8 December, "Marble Floor")

When I wrote these words I was thinking of Peter and of the whole reality of the ministerial priesthood, and trying to bring out the profound significance of this liturgical prostration. In lying prostrate on the floor in the form of a cross before one's ordination, in accepting in one's own life—like Peter—the cross of Christ and becoming with the Apostle a "floor" for our brothers and sisters, one finds the ultimate meaning of all priestly spirituality.

My First Mass

Having been ordained a priest on the feast of All Saints, I celebrated my First Mass on All Souls Day, 2 November 1946. On that day every priest may celebrate three Masses for the benefit of the faithful. So in a sense I celebrated three "first" Masses. It was a deeply moving experience. I celebrated the three Masses in the crypt of Saint Leonard, which, in Wawel Cathedral at Cracow, is the front part of the so-called episcopal cathedral of Herman. Today the crypt is part of the underground complex where the royal tombs are located. I chose this place for the celebration of my first Masses in order to express my spiritual bonds with those buried in that Cathedral. Given its history, it is a monument without parallel. More than any other Polish church, Wawel Cathedral is full of historical and theological significance. The kings of Poland are buried there, beginning with Władysław Łokietek: there they were crowned and there they were laid to rest. All who visit the Cathedral find themselves immersed in the nation's history.

This, then, was why I wanted to celebrate my first Masses in the *crypt of Saint Leonard:* I wanted to express my special spiritual bond with the history of Poland, a history symbolized by the hill of Wawel. But there was more. My choice also had a particular *theological significance.* As I said, I had been ordained the day before, on the Solemnity of All Saints, when the Church gives liturgical expression to the reality of the Communion of Saints—*communio sanctorum.* The saints are those who, having accepted the Paschal Mystery of Christ in faith, now await the final resurrection.

All those whose mortal remains rest in the tombs of Wawel Cathedral lie there in expectation of the resurrection. The whole Cathedral thus seems to echo the words of the Apostles' Creed: "I believe in the resurrection of the body and life everlasting." This truth of faith also sheds light on the history of the nation. All those people are "great spirits" who led the nation through the ages. In their ranks are found not only sovereigns and their consorts, or Bishops and Cardinals, but also poets, great masters of language, who were extremely influential in my education as a Christian and a patriot.

Few people were at those first Masses celebrated on the hill of Wawel: among others, I remember my godmother Maria Wiadrowska, my mother's elder sister. The altar server was Mieczysław Maliński, who in a way made present the spirit and person of Jan Tyranowski, at the time already seriously ill.

Later, as a priest and Bishop, I always visited the crypt of Saint Leonard with great emotion. How I would have liked to celebrate Mass there on the fiftieth anniversary of my priestly ordination!

Among the People of God

Other "first Masses" followed: in the parish church of Saint Stanislaus Kostka at Dębniki and the following Sunday in Wadowice, at the Church of the Presentation of the Mother of God. I also celebrated a Mass at the Confession of Saint Stanislaus in Wawel Cathedral for my friends in the rhapsodic theater and for the clandestine group Unia ("Union"), to which I was linked during the occupation.

V

Rome

November went by quickly: it was now time *to leave for Rome.* When the set day arrived, I boarded the train with great excitement. With me was Stanisław Starowieyski, a younger colleague who had been sent to take his whole course of theological studies in Rome. For the first time I was leaving the borders of my homeland. From the window of the moving train I looked at cities known previously only from my geography books. For the first time I saw Prague, Nuremberg, Strasbourg, and Paris, where we stopped as guests of the Polish Seminary on the rue des Irlandais. We stayed there only briefly, since time was pressing, and reached Rome in the last days of November. Here we first enjoyed the hospitality of the Pallottine Fathers. I remember the first Sunday after our arrival, when I went with Stanisław Starowieyski to Saint Peter's Basilica and attended the Pope's solemn veneration of a newly proclaimed Blessed. From afar I saw Pope Pius XII being carried on the *sedia gestatoria.* The Pope's participation in a beatification in those days was limited to the recitation of a prayer to the new Blessed, while the rite itself was celebrated in the morning by one of the cardinals. This tradition was changed, beginning with Maximilian Maria Kolbe, when—in October 1971—Paul VI personally celebrated the beatification of the Polish martyr of Auschwitz at a solemn Mass concelebrated by Cardinal Wyszyński and the Polish Bishops. I too had the joy of taking part.

"Learning Rome"

I will never forget my feelings during those first "Roman" days of mine, when in 1946 I began to get to know the Eternal City. *I enrolled in the two-year doctoral program at the Angelicum.* The Dean of the Theology Faculty was Father Mario Luigi Ciappi, O.P., later theologian of the Papal Household and Cardinal.

Father Karol Kozłowski, Rector of the Cracow Seminary, had told me a number of times that for those fortunate enough to study in the capital of Christendom, it was more important to *"learn Rome itself"* than simply to study (after all, a doctorate in theology can be gotten elsewhere!). I tried to follow his advice. I came to Rome with an eager desire to see the Eternal City, beginning with the catacombs. And so it happened. Together with friends from the Belgian College, where I lived, I was able systematically to explore the city under the guidance of those who knew its monuments and history. During the Christmas and Easter holidays we were able to visit other Italian cities. I remember my first vacation, when, using as our guide a book written by the Danish author Jørgensen, we went off to discover the places associated with the life of Saint Francis.

But Rome was always *the center of our experience.*

Wadowice. Parish church of the Presentation
of the Blessed Virgin Mary.

Wadowice. Childhood home of Pope John Paul II.

Cracow. *Collegium Maius* of the Jagiellonian University.

Cracow. Entrance of the Archbishop's Residence.

Kalwaria Zebrzydowska, shrine of
the Blessed Virgin Mary.

Cracow. Steps leading to 10 Tyniecka Street.

Cracow. Facade of the Major Seminary.

Cracow. Wawel Cathedral. Altar of Saint Hedwig,
Queen of Poland.

Cracow. Church of the Albertine Sisters.
Ecce Homo by Brother Saint Albert.

Cracow. Archbishop's Residence. Altar in the Chapel.

Cracow. Wawel Cathedral. Crypt of Saint Leonard.

Niegowić. Parish church of the
Assumption of the Blessed Virgin Mary.

Cracow. Wawel Cathedral. Confession of
Saint Stanislaus, Bishop and Martyr.

Cracow. Parish church of Saint Florian.

Cracow. Wawel Cathedral.

Rome. Bernini colonnade and dome of Saint Peter's.

I would set off every day from the Belgian College, at 26 via del Quirinale, to attend lectures at the *Angelicum*. I would always make a stop at the Jesuit church of Sant'Andrea al Quirinale, where the relics of Saint Stanislaus Kostka are enshrined. Saint Stanislaus had lived in the novitiate next door and died there. I remember that among the visitors to his tomb there were many seminarians from the *Germanicum*, easily recognizable by their characteristic red cassocks. At the heart of Christendom, and in the light of the saints, people from different nations would come together, as if to foreshadow, beyond the tragic war which had left such a deep mark on us, a world no longer divided.

Pastoral Perspectives

My priesthood and my theological and pastoral formation *were part of my Roman experience from the beginning.* The two years of study, completed in 1948 with the doctorate, were a time when I made every effort to "learn Rome." The Belgian College helped to plant my priesthood firmly, day after day, in the life of the capital of Christendom. It enabled me to come into contact with certain innovative forms of apostolate then developing in the Church. Here I am thinking especially of meeting Father Jozef Cardijn, founder of the Young Christian Worker movement and future cardinal, who came to the College from time to time to meet the priest-students and to speak with us about the meaning of the human experience of physical labor. To a certain extent, I had already been prepared for this by my work in the stone quarry and in the water purification facility of the Solvay plant. But in Rome I was able to grasp more fully how much the priesthood is linked to pastoral ministry and the apostolate of the laity. A close connection, or, better, a mutual correlation, exists between priestly service and the lay apostolate. As I reflected on these pastoral issues, I came to appreciate ever more clearly the meaning and value of the ministerial priesthood.

The European Horizon

My experience at the Belgian College was subsequently broadened through direct contact not only with Belgium itself, but also with France and Holland. With the consent of Cardinal Sapieha, Father Stanisław Starowieyski and I were able to visit those countries during the summer holiday of 1947. There I came to appreciate the broader European context. In Paris, where I stayed at the Polish Seminary, I came into contact with the worker-priest movement, the issues raised by Fathers Henri Godin and Yvan Daniel in their book *La France, pays de mission?*, and the work being done in the missions on the outskirts of Paris, especially in the parish run by Father Michonneau. These experiences, in my first and second years of priesthood, proved enormously important to me.

With the help of friends, especially the parents of the late Father Alfred Delmé, Stanisław Starowieyski and I were able to spend ten days in Holland. I was impressed by the vigor of the Church and the pastoral ministry in that country, its active organizations and lively ecclesial communities.

From different and complementary angles, I was coming to an ever greater appreciation of *Western Europe:* the Europe of the postwar period, a Europe of splendid Gothic cathedrals and yet a Europe threatened by increasing secularization. I understood the challenge that this posed to the Church, and the need to confront this impending danger through new forms of pastoral activity open to a broader participation by the laity.

In the Midst of Immigrants

But it was in Belgium that I spent most of my summer holidays. In the month of September I had charge of *the Polish Catholic mission* among the miners in the area around Charleroi. This proved a very fruitful experience. This was my first visit to a coal mine and I was able personally to witness the hard work done by miners. I visited the families of Polish immigrants, spoke with them, met the young people and children. I was always shown kindness and warmth, as when I worked at Solvay.

The Figure of
Saint John Mary Vianney

On my way back from Belgium to Rome, I was able to *spend some time in Ars.* It was the end of October 1947, the feast of Christ the King. With great emotion I visited the little old church where Saint John Vianney heard confessions, taught catechism, and gave his homilies. It was an unforgettable experience for me. From my seminary years I had been impressed by the figure of the Curé d'Ars, especially after reading his biography by Monsignor Trochu. Saint John Mary Vianney astonishes us because in him we can see the power of grace working through human limitations. It was his *heroic service in the confessional* which particularly struck me. That humble priest, who would hear confessions more than ten hours a day, eating little and sleeping only a few hours, was able, at a difficult moment in history, to inspire a kind of spiritual revolution in France, and not only there. Thousands of people passed through Ars and knelt at his confessional. Against the background of attacks on the Church and the clergy in the nineteenth century, his witness was truly revolutionary.

My encounter with this saintly figure confirmed me in *the conviction that a priest fulfills an essential part of his mission through the confessional*—by voluntarily "making himself a prisoner of the confessional." Many times, as I heard confessions in my first parish at Niegowić and then in Cracow, my thoughts would turn to this unforgettable experience. I have always tried to maintain this link to the confessional, both during my years of teaching in Cracow, when I would hear confessions mainly in the Basilica of the Assumption of the Blessed Virgin Mary, and now in Rome, even if only symbolically, when every year on Good Friday I sit in the confessional in Saint Peter's Basilica.

Heartfelt Gratitude

I cannot conclude these reflections without expressing heartfelt gratitude to all *the members of the Belgian College in Rome*, the superiors and my companions at the time, of whom many have already died. I am especially grateful to the Rector, Father Maximilien de Furstenberg, who later became a cardinal. How can I fail to remember that during the conclave of 1978 Cardinal de Furstenberg came up to me at a certain moment and uttered the significant words *Dominus adest et vocat te?* It was like a subtle and mysterious completion of the role he had played, as Rector of the Belgian College, in my priestly formation.

My Return to Poland

At the beginning of July 1948 I defended my doctoral dissertation at the *Angelicum* and then immediately left for Poland. As I mentioned earlier, I had made every effort during my two-year stay in the Eternal City to "learn" Rome: the Rome of the catacombs, the Rome of the martyrs, the Rome of Peter and Paul, the Rome of the confessors of the faith. I often think back on those years with great emotion. As I left, I took with me not only *a much broader theological education but also a strengthened priesthood and a more profound vision of the Church.* That period of intense study close to the tombs of the Apostles had given me much, from every point of view.

Of course I could add many other details about that decisive experience. But I would sum it all up by saying that in Rome the early years of my priesthood *had taken on both a European and a universal dimension.* I returned from Rome to Cracow with that sense of *the universality of the priestly mission* which found authoritative expression at the Second Vatican Council, particularly in the Dogmatic Constitution on the Church, *Lumen Gentium.* Not only Bishops, but every priest must be personally concerned for the whole Church and should in some way feel responsible for the whole Church.

VI

Niegowić: a Country Parish

As soon as I reached Cracow, I went to the Metropolitan Curia to receive my first "assignment," the so-called *aplikata.* The Archbishop was then in Rome, but he had left written instructions. I accepted the appointment with joy. Immediately I inquired how to get to Niegowić and made plans to be there on the day appointed. I went from Cracow to Gdów by bus, and from there a local man gave me a ride in his cart to the village of Marszowice; from there he advised me to take a shortcut through the fields on foot. I could already see the church of Niegowić in the distance. It was harvest time. I walked through the fields of grain with the crops in part already reaped, and in part still waving in the wind. When I finally reached the territory of Niegowić parish, I knelt down and kissed the ground. It was a gesture I had learned from Saint John Mary Vianney. In the church I made a visit to the Blessed Sacrament and then introduced myself to the parish priest, Monsignor Kazimierz Buzała, dean of Niepołomice and parish priest of Niegowić, who welcomed me very cordially and after a brief conversation showed me the curate's quarters.

And so I began my pastoral work in my *first parish*. It lasted for a year and consisted of the usual tasks assigned to a curate and religion teacher. I was put in charge of five elementary schools in the villages belonging to the parish of Niegowić. People would take me there by cart or carriage. I remember the friendliness of the teachers and parishioners. The classes were all quite different: some were well behaved and quiet, others very lively. Even today I sometimes think back on the recollected silence which prevailed in the classrooms when, during Lent, I would speak about the Lord's Passion.

At that time the parish of Niegowić was preparing

to celebrate the fiftieth anniversary of the ordination of the parish priest. As the old church was no longer adequate for the needs of the parish, the parishioners decided that the best gift for the jubilarian would be to build a new church. But I was soon taken away from that wonderful community.

At Saint Florian's in Cracow

And so, after a year, I was transferred to the parish of Saint Florian in Cracow. The parish priest, Monsignor Tadeusz Kurowski, entrusted me with teaching catechism to the senior classes of the secondary school and providing pastoral care to the students at the university. At that time the university chaplaincy in Cracow was centered at Saint Anne's Church, but with the addition of new faculties of study it became necessary to create a new center at Saint Florian's parish. There I began to give talks to the young people at the university; every Thursday I would speak to them about fundamental problems concerning the existence of God and the spiritual nature of the human soul. These were extremely important issues, given the militant atheism being promoted by the communist regime.

Scholarly Work

During the vacation of 1951, after two years of work in Saint Florian's parish, Archbishop Eugeniusz Baziak, who had succeeded Cardinal Sapieha as Archbishop of Cracow, directed me towards scholarly work. I was to prepare for the diploma qualifying me to teach ethics and moral theology. This meant that I would have less time for the pastoral work so dear to me. This was a sacrifice, but from that time on I was always resolved that my dedication to the study of theology and philosophy would not lead me to "forget" that I was a priest; rather it would help me to become one ever more fully.

VII

*To the Church
in Poland, Thank You!*

In this jubilee testimony how can I fail to express *my
gratitude to the whole Church in Poland,* in which my priesthood was born and developed? It is a Church marked
by a thousand-year-old heritage of faith, a Church
which down the centuries has produced many saints
and blesseds, and is entrusted to the patronage of
two saintly Bishops and Martyrs: Adalbert and
Stanislaus. It is a Church closely linked to the Polish
people and their culture, a Church which has always
upheld and defended that people, especially in the
tragic periods of its history. It is also a Church

which has experienced severe trials in this century: it had to endure a dramatic struggle for survival against *two totalitarian systems:* the regime inspired by the *Nazi ideology* during the Second World War and then, in the long postwar period, a *communist dictatorship* and its militant atheism.

From both trials the Polish Church emerged victorious, thanks to the sacrifices of Bishops, priests and countless lay people; thanks too to the Polish family, which is "strong in God." Among the Bishops of the war period I cannot fail to mention the staunch figure of the Prince Metropolitan of Cracow, Adam Stefan Sapieha, and, among those of the postwar years, that of the Servant of God Stefan, Cardinal Wyszyński. The Polish Church is a *Church which has defended man,* his dignity and his fundamental rights; it is a Church which *has fought courageously* for the right of believers to profess their faith. And it is a Church which has remained extraordinarily dynamic, despite the difficulties and obstacles which stood in its path.

In this intense spiritual climate my mission as a priest and Bishop gradually took shape. The two totalitarian systems which tragically marked our century—Nazism on the one hand, marked by the horrors of war and the concentration camps, and communism on the other, with its regime of oppression and terror—I came to know, so to speak, from within. And so it is easy to understand my deep concern for the dignity of every human person and the need to respect human rights, beginning with the *right to life*. This concern was shaped in the first years of my priesthood and has grown stronger with time. It is also easy to understand my concern for the family and for young people. These concerns are all interwoven; they developed precisely as a result of those tragic experiences.

The Presbyterate of Cracow

On the fiftieth anniversary of my priestly ordination my thoughts go in a special way to the presbyterate of the *Church of Cracow*, of which I was a member as a priest and then its head as Archbishop. So many outstanding parish priests and curates come to mind that it would take too long to mention them one by one. Then and now, bonds of deep friendship have united me to many of them. The example of their holiness and pastoral zeal has been immensely edifying to me. Certainly they have had a profound influence on my priesthood. From them I have learned what it means in practice to be a pastor.

I am deeply convinced of the *decisive role that the diocesan presbyterate plays in the personal life of every priest.* The community of priests, rooted in a true *sacramental fraternity,* is a setting second to none for spiritual and pastoral formation. The priest, as a rule, cannot do without this community. The presbyterate helps him in his growth towards holiness and is a sure support in times of difficulty. On the occasion of my Golden Jubilee, how can I fail to express my gratitude to all the priests of the Archdiocese of Cracow for everything that they have contributed to my priesthood?

The Gift of Lay People

At this time I also think of all the lay people whom the Lord has had me meet in my mission as priest and Bishop. They have been a *unique gift* to me, and I thank Providence for them every day. They are so numerous that it is impossible to list them by name, but I carry them all in my heart, for each one of them has made his or her own contribution to the growth of my priesthood. In one way or another they have shown me the way, helping me to understand my ministry better and to live it more fully. My frequent contacts with lay men and women have always proved profitable and instructive. Among them were ordinary workers, men and women of art and culture, and great scholars. These contacts have given rise to good friendships, many of which I still enjoy today. Thanks to these people, my pastoral work was able to increase; I was able to overcome barriers and to move in circles which otherwise would have been very difficult to reach.

In effect, I have always been very aware of the urgent need for the *apostolate of the laity* in the Church.

When the Second Vatican Council spoke of the vocation and mission of lay people in the Church and the world, I rejoiced: what the Council was teaching corresponded to the convictions which had guided my activity ever since the first years of my priestly ministry.

VIII

Who Is the Priest?

In this personal testimony, I also feel the need to go beyond the mere recollection of events and individuals in order to take a deeper look and to search out, as it were, the mystery which for fifty years has accompanied and enfolded me.

What does it mean to be a priest? According to Saint Paul, it means above all to be *a steward of the mysteries of God:* "This is how one should regard us, as servants of Christ and stewards of the mysteries of God. Now it is required of stewards that they be found trustworthy" (I Cor 4:1–2). The word "steward" cannot be replaced by any other. It is deeply rooted in the Gospel: it brings to mind the parable of the faithful steward and the unfaithful one (cf. Lk 12:41–48). The steward is not the owner, but the one to whom the owner entrusts his goods so that he will manage them justly and responsibly. In exactly the same way the priest receives from Christ the treasures of salvation, in order duly to distribute them among the people to whom he is sent. These treasures are those of faith. The priest is thus a man of the word of God, a man of sacrament, a man of the "mystery of faith." Through faith he draws near to the invisible treasures which constitute the inheritance of the world's Redemption by the Son of God. No one may consider himself the "owner" of these treasures; they are meant for us all. But, by reason of what Christ laid down, the priest has the task of administering them.

Admirabile Commercium!

The priestly vocation is a mystery. *It is the mystery of a "wondrous exchange"—admirabile commercium—*between

God and man. A man offers his humanity to Christ, so that Christ may use him as an instrument of salvation, making him as it were into another Christ. Unless we grasp the mystery of this "exchange," we will not understand how it can be that a young man, hearing the words "Follow me!," can give up everything for Christ, in the certainty that if he follows this path he will find complete personal fulfillment.

In our world, is there any greater fulfillment of our humanity than to be able to re-present every day *in persona Christi* the redemptive sacrifice, the same sacrifice which Christ offered on the Cross? In this sacrifice, on the one hand, the very mystery of the Trinity is present in the most profound way, and, on the other hand, the entire created universe is "united" (cf. Eph 1:10). The Eucharist is also celebrated in order to offer "on the altar of the whole earth the world's work and suffering," in the beautiful expression of Teilhard de Chardin. This is why in the thanksgiving after Holy Mass the Old Testament canticle of the three young men is recited: *Benedicite omnia opera Domini Domino.* For in the Eucharist all creatures seen and unseen, and man in particular, bless God as Creator and Father; they bless him with the words and the action of Christ, the Son of God.

The Priest and the Eucharist

"I thank you, Father, Lord of heaven and earth, that you have hidden these things from the wise and understanding and revealed them to babes. . . . No one knows who the Son is except the Father, or who the Father is except the Son and any one to whom the Son chooses to reveal him" (Lk 10:21–22). These words of Saint Luke's Gospel lead us to the heart of the mystery of Christ and enable us to draw near to the mystery of the Eucharist. In the Eucharist, the Son, who is of one being with the Father, the One whom only the Father knows, offers himself in sacrifice to the Father for humanity and for all creation. In the Eucharist Christ gives back to the Father everything that has come from him. Thus there is brought about a profound *mystery of justice on the part of the creature towards the Creator.* Man needs to honor his

Creator by offering to him, in an act of thanksgiving and praise, all that he has received. *Man must never lose sight of this debt*, which he alone, among all other earthly realities, is capable of acknowledging and paying back as the one creature made in God's own image and likeness. At the same time, given his creaturely limitations and sinful condition, man would be incapable of making this act of justice towards the Creator, had not Christ himself, the Son who is of one being with the Father and also true man, first given us the Eucharist.

The priesthood, in its deepest reality, is *the priesthood of Christ*. It is Christ who offers himself, his Body and Blood, in sacrifice to God the Father, and by this sacrifice makes righteous in the Father's eyes all mankind and, indirectly, all creation. The priest, in his daily celebration of the Eucharist, goes to the very heart of this mystery. For this reason the celebration of the Eucharist must be the most important moment of the priest's day, the center of his life.

In Persona Christi

The words which we repeat at the end of the Preface—"Blessed is he who comes in the name of the Lord"—take us back to the dramatic events of Palm Sunday. Christ goes to Jerusalem to face the bloody sacrifice of Good Friday. But the day before, at the Last Supper, he institutes the sacrament of this sacrifice. Over the bread and wine he says the words of consecration: "This is my Body, which will be given up for you. . . . This is the cup of my Blood, the Blood of the new and everlasting covenant. It will be shed for you and for all so that sins may be forgiven. Do this in memory of me."

What kind of a "memorial" is this? We know that this term must be given a weighty significance, one which goes far beyond mere historical remembrance. Here we are speaking of a "memorial" in the biblical sense, a memorial which *makes present* the event itself. It is *memory* and *presence.* The secret of this miracle is the action of the Holy Spirit, whom the priest invokes when he extends his hands over the gifts of bread and wine: "Let *your Spirit* come upon these gifts to make them holy, so that they may become for us the Body and Blood of our Lord Jesus Christ." Thus it is not merely the priest who recalls the events of Christ's Passion, Death, and Resurrection; it is also the Holy Spirit who enables this event to be made present on the altar through the ministry of the priest. The priest truly acts *in persona Christi*. What Christ accomplished on the altar of the Cross and what earlier still he had instituted as a sacrament in the Upper Room, the priest now renews by the power of the Holy Spirit. At this moment the priest is as it were embraced by the power of the Holy Spirit, and the words which he utters have the same efficacy as those spoken by Christ at the Last Supper.

Mysterium Fidei

At Holy Mass, after the consecration, the priest says the words *Mysterium fidei, Let us proclaim the mystery of faith!* These words refer of course to the Eucharist. In a way, however, they also concern the priesthood. There can be no Eucharist without the priesthood, just as there can be no priesthood without the Eucharist. Not only is the ministerial priesthood closely linked to the Eucharist, but the common priesthood of all the baptized is also rooted in this mystery. To the celebrant's words the people reply: "When we eat this bread and drink this cup we proclaim your death, Lord Jesus, until you come in glory." As the Second Vatican Council reminded us, the faithful, by their sharing in the Eucharistic Sacrifice, become witnesses of the Crucified and Risen Christ and commit themselves to living his threefold mission—as priest, prophet, and king—which they received at Baptism.

The priest, as steward of the "mysteries of God," is at the service of the common priesthood of the faithful. By proclaiming the word and celebrating the sacraments, especially the Eucharist, he makes the whole People of God ever more aware of its share in Christ's priesthood, and at the same time encourages it to live that priesthood to the full. When, after the consecration, he says the words *Mysterium fidei*, all are invited to ponder the rich existential meaning of this proclamation, which refers to the mystery of Christ, the Eucharist, and the priesthood.

Is this not the deepest reason behind the priestly vocation? Certainly it is already fully present at the time of ordination, but it needs to be interiorized and deepened for the rest of the priest's life. Only in this way can a priest discover in depth the great treasure which has been entrusted to him. Fifty years after my ordination, I can say that in the words *Mysterium fidei* we find ever more each day the meaning of our own priesthood. Here is the measure of the gift which is the priesthood, and here is also the measure of the response which this gift demands. *The gift is constantly growing!* And this is something wonderful. It is wonderful that a man can never say that he has fully responded to the gift. It remains both a gift and a task: always! To be conscious of this is essential if we are to live our own priesthood to the full.

Christ, Priest and Victim

The truth about Christ's priesthood has always struck me in an extraordinarily eloquent way in the

Litany which used to be recited in the seminary at Cracow, especially on the eve of a priestly ordination. I am referring to the *Litany of Our Lord Jesus Christ, Priest and Victim.* What profound reflections it prompted! In the Sacrifice of the Cross, made present anew in every Eucharist, Christ offers himself for the salvation of the world. The invocations of the Litany call to mind the many aspects of this mystery. They come back to me with all the rich symbolism of the biblical images with which they are interwoven. When I repeat them, it is in Latin, the language in which I recited them at the seminary and then so often in later years:

Iesu, Sacerdos et Victima,
Iesu, Sacerdos in aeternum secundum ordinem
        Melchisedech,
Iesu, Pontifex ex hominibus assumpte,
Iesu, Pontifex pro hominibus constitute,
Iesu, Pontifex futurorum bonorum,
Iesu, Pontifex fidelis et misericors,
Iesu, Pontifex qui dilexisti nos et lavisti nos a peccatis
        in sanguine tuo,

Iesu, Pontifex qui tradidisti temetipsum Deo
oblationem et hostiam,
Iesu, Hostia sancta et immaculata,
Iesu, Hostia in qua habemus fiduciam
et accessum ad Deum,
Iesu, Hostia vivens in saecula saeculorum. *

What theological depth is present in these expressions! They are *invocations deeply rooted in Sacred Scripture,* especially in the Letter to the Hebrews. We need only reread this passage: "Christ . . . as a high priest of the good things to come . . . entered once for all into the Holy Place, taking not the blood of goats and calves but his own blood, thus securing an eternal redemption. For if the sprinkling of defiled persons with the blood of goats and bulls . . . sanctifies for the purification of the flesh, how much more shall the blood of Christ, who through the eternal Spirit offered himself without blemish to God, purify our conscience from dead works to serve the living

---

* The full text of the Litany can be found in the Appendix.

God" (Heb 9:11–14). *Christ is a priest because he is the Redeemer of the world.* The priesthood of all presbyters is part of the mystery of the Redemption. This truth about Redemption and the Redeemer has been central to me; it has been with me all these years, it has permeated all my pastoral experiences, and it has continued to reveal new riches to me.

In these fifty years of priestly life, I have come to realize that the Redemption, the price which had to be paid for sin, entails *a renewed discovery, a kind of a "new creation" of the whole created order:* the rediscovery of man as a person, of man created by God as male and female, a rediscovery of the deepest truth about all man's works, his culture and civilization, about all his achievements and creative abilities.

After I was elected Pope, my first spiritual impulse was to turn to Christ the Redeemer. This was the origin of the Encyclical Letter *Redemptor Hominis.* As I reflect on all these events, I see ever more clearly the close link between the message of that Encyclical and everything that is found in the heart of man through his sharing in Christ's priesthood.

IX

Being a Priest Today

Fifty years as a priest is a long time. How much has happened in this half-century of history! New problems, new lifestyles, and new challenges have appeared. And so it is natural to ask: what does it mean to be a priest *today*, in this time of constant change, as we approach the Third Millennium?

Certainly the priest, together with the whole Church, is part of the times in which he lives; he needs to be attentive and sympathetic, but also critical and watchful, with regard to historical developments. The Council has pointed to the possibility and need for an authentic renewal, in complete fidelity to the word of God and Tradition. But I am convinced that a priest, committed as he is to this necessary pastoral renewal, should at the same time have no fear of being "behind the times," because the human "today" of every priest is included in the "today" of Christ the Redeemer. For every priest, in every age, the greatest task is each day to discover his own priestly "today" in the "today" of Christ to which the Letter to the Hebrews refers. This "today" of Christ is immersed in the whole of history—in the past and future of the world, of every human being and of every priest. "Jesus Christ is the same yesterday and today and forever" (Heb 13:8). If we immerse our human and priestly "today" in the "today" of Jesus Christ, there is no danger that we will become out-of-date, belonging to "yesterday." Christ is the measure of every age. In his divine, human, and priestly "today," the conflict between "traditionalism" and "progressivism"—once so hotly debated—finds its ultimate resolution.

Humanity's Profound Expectations

If we take a close look at what contemporary men and women expect from priests, we will see that, in the end, they have but one great expectation: *they are thirsting for Christ.* Everything else—their economic, social, and political needs—can be met by any number of other people. From the priest they ask for Christ! And from him they have the right to receive Christ, above all through the proclamation of the word. As the Council teaches, priests "have as their primary duty the proclamation of the Gospel of God to all" *(Presbyterorum Ordinis, 4).* But this proclamation seeks to have man encounter Jesus, especially in the mystery of the Eucharist, the living heart of the Church and of priestly life. The priest has a mysterious, awesome power over the Eucharistic Body of Christ. By reason of this power he becomes the steward of the greatest treasure of the Redemption, for he gives people the Redeemer in person. Celebrating the Eucharist is the most sublime and most sacred function of every priest. As for me, from the very first years of my priesthood, the celebration of the Eucharist has been not only my most sacred duty, but above all my soul's deepest need.

A Minister of Mercy

As the steward of the *Sacrament of Reconciliation,* the priest fulfills the command given by Christ to the Apostles after his Resurrection: "Receive the Holy Spirit. If you forgive the sins of any, they are forgiven; if you retain the sins of any, they are retained" (Jn 20:22–23). The priest is the witness and instrument of divine mercy! How important in his life is the ministry of the confessional! It is in the confessional that *his spiritual fatherhood* is realized in the fullest way. It is in the confessional that every priest becomes a witness of the great miracles which divine mercy works in souls which receive the grace of conversion. It is necessary, however, that every priest at the service of his brothers and sisters in the confessional should experience this same divine mercy by going regularly to confession himself and by receiving spiritual direction.

As a steward of God's mysteries, the priest is a special *witness to the Invisible* in the world. For he is a steward of invisible and priceless treasures belonging to the spiritual and supernatural order.

A Man in Contact with God

As a steward of these treasures, the priest is always in special contact with *the holiness of God.* "Holy, holy, holy Lord, God of power and might, heaven and earth are full of your glory." God's majesty is the majesty of holiness. In the priesthood a man is as it were raised up to the sphere of this holiness; in some way he reaches the heights to which the Prophet Isaiah was once exalted. And it is precisely this vision of the Prophet which is echoed in the Eucharistic Liturgy: *Sanctus, Sanctus, Sanctus, Dominus Deus Sabaoth. Pleni sunt caeli et terra gloria tua. Hosanna in excelsis.*

At the same time, the priest experiences daily and continually the descent of God's holiness upon man: *Benedictus qui venit in nomine Domini.* With these words the crowds in Jerusalem greeted Christ as he came into the city to accomplish the sacrifice which brought Redemption to the world. Transcendent holiness, which is in a sense "outside the world," becomes in Christ a holiness which is "in the world." It becomes the holiness of the Paschal Mystery.

Called to Holiness

Constantly in contact with the holiness of God, the priest must himself become holy. His very ministry commits him to a way of life inspired by the radicalism of the Gospel. This explains his particular need to live in the spirit of the evangelical counsels of chastity, poverty, and obedience. Here we also see the special fittingness of celibacy. We also see the particular need for prayer in his life: prayer finds its source in God's holiness and is at the same time our response to this holiness. I once wrote: "Prayer makes the priest and through prayer the priest becomes himself." Before all else the priest must indeed be a *man of prayer*, convinced that time devoted to personal encounter with God is always spent in the best way possible. This not only benefits him; it also benefits his apostolic work.

While the Second Vatican Council speaks of the *universal* call to holiness, in the case of the priest we must speak of a *special* call to holiness. *Christ needs holy priests!* Today's world demands holy priests! Only a holy priest can become, in an increasingly secularized world, a resounding witness to Christ and his Gospel. And only thus can a priest become a guide for men and women and a teacher of holiness. People, especially the young, are looking for such guides. A priest can be a guide and teacher only to the extent that he becomes an authentic witness!

Cura Animarum

My now long experience, amid so many different situations, has confirmed my conviction that *priestly holiness alone is the soil which can nourish an effective pastoral activity, a true "cura animarum."* The truest secret of authentic pastoral success does not lie in material means, much less in sophisticated programs. The lasting results of pastoral endeavors are born of the holiness of the priest. This is the foundation! Needless to say, training, study, and updating are indispensable; in short, an adequate preparation which enables one to respond to urgent needs and to discern *pastoral priorities.* But it can also be said that priorities depend on circumstances, and every priest is called to identify and pursue them under the authority of his Bishop and in harmony with the directives of the universal Church. In my own life I have identified these priorities in the lay apostolate and particularly in the pastoral care of the family—an area in which lay people themselves have helped me so much—in youth ministry and in serious dialogue with the world of learning and culture. All this has been reflected in my scholarly and literary activity. This was the origin of my study *Love and Responsibility* and, among others, the literary work *The Jeweler's Shop,* which is subtitled *Meditations on the Sacrament of Marriage.*

An inescapable priority today is that of preferential concern for the poor, the marginalized, and immigrants. The priest must be truly a "father" to such people. Material means are of course indispensable, such as those offered by modern technology. But the real secret is always the priest's holiness of life, which finds expression in prayer and meditation, in a spirit of sacrifice and in missionary zeal. When I think back on my years of pastoral ministry as priest and Bishop, I become more and more convinced of how true and fundamental this is.

A Man of the Word

I have already mentioned that, to be an authentic guide of the community and a true steward of the mysteries of God, the priest is also called to be a *man of God's word*, a generous and tireless evangelizer. Today the urgency of this is seen even more clearly in the light of the immense task of the "new evangelization."

After so many years of being a minister of the word, which especially during my papacy has brought me as a pilgrim to every part of the world, I cannot fail to make further considerations regarding this dimension of priestly life. This is a demanding dimension, since people today look to priests for the "lived" word before they look to them for the "proclaimed" word. The priest must "live by the word." But at the same time, he will try to be *intellectually prepared* to know the word in depth and to proclaim it effectively. In our day, marked as it is by a high degree of specialization in almost all areas of life, intellectual formation is extremely important. Such formation makes it possible to engage in a serious and creative dialogue with contemporary thought. Study of the humanities and of philosophy and a knowledge of theology are the paths to this intellectual formation, which then needs to be continued for the rest of one's life. In order to be authentically formative, study needs to be constantly accompanied by prayer, meditation, and the invocation of the gifts of the Holy Spirit: wisdom, understanding, counsel, fortitude, knowledge, piety, and the fear of the Lord. Saint Thomas Aquinas explains how, with the gifts of the Holy Spirit, a person's whole spiritual being becomes responsive to God's light, not only the light of knowledge but also the inspiration of love. I have prayed for the gifts of the Holy Spirit since my youth and I continue to do so.

Scholarly Study

But of course Saint Thomas also teaches that "infused knowledge," which is the fruit of a special intervention by the Holy Spirit, does not free us from the duty of gaining "acquired knowledge."

In my case, as I have already said, immediately after my priestly ordination I was sent to Rome to complete my studies. Later, at the behest of my Archbishop, I had to devote myself to scholarly work as a professor of ethics at the Theological Faculty of Cracow and at the Catholic University of Lublin. These studies resulted in my doctorate on Saint John of the Cross and then the dissertation on Max Scheler which qualified me for university teaching: specifically, I wrote on the contribution which Scheler's phenomenological type of ethical system can make to the development of moral theology. This research benefited me greatly. My previous Aristotelian-

Thomistic formation was enriched by the phenomenological method, and this made it possible for me to
undertake a number of creative studies. I am thinking
above all of my book *The Acting Person.* In this way I
took part in the contemporary movement of philo-
sophical personalism, and my studies were able to
bear fruit in my pastoral work. I have often noticed
how many of the ideas developed in these studies
have helped me in my meetings with individuals and
with great numbers of the faithful during my apostolic visits. My formation within the cultural horizon
of personalism also gave me a deeper awareness of
how each individual is a unique person. I think that
this awareness is very important for every priest.

Dialogue with Contemporary Thought

Thanks to meetings and discussions with experts in
the natural sciences, with physicists and biologists as
well as with historians, I have learned to appreciate
the importance of those other branches of knowledge

which involve the scientific disciplines; these are likewise capable of attaining the truth from different perspectives. The splendor of the truth—*Veritatis Splendor*—constantly needs to accompany them, enabling people to meet, to exchange ideas, and to enrich one another. I brought with me from Cracow to Rome the tradition of periodic interdisciplinary meetings; these take place regularly during the summer at Castel Gandolfo. I try to be faithful to this good habit.

"Labia sacerdotum scientiam custodiant" (cf. Mal 2:7). I like to recall these words of the Prophet Malachi, which are found in the *Litany of Christ, Priest and Victim,* because they represent a kind of program for the one called to be a minister of the word. He must always be *a man of knowledge* in the highest and most religious sense of the term. He must possess and pass on that "knowledge of God" which is not a mere deposit of doctrinal truths but a personal and living experience of the Mystery, in the sense spoken of by the Gospel of Saint John in the great priestly prayer: "This is eternal life, that they *know* you, the only true God, and Jesus Christ whom you have sent" (17:3).

X

To My Brothers
in the Priesthood

As I come to the end of this testimony to my priestly vocation, *I wish to address all my brothers in the priesthood:* each and every one of them! I do so in the words of Saint Peter: "Brethren, be the more zealous to confirm your call and election, for if you do this you will never fall" (2 Pet 1:10). Love your priesthood! Be faithful to the end! Learn to see in your priesthood the Gospel treasure for which it is worth *giving up everything* (cf. Mt 13:44).

In a special way I turn to those of you who are experiencing a time of difficulty or even a crisis in your vocation. I would like my personal testimony—the testimony of a priest and the Bishop of Rome, who is celebrating the Golden Jubilee of his ordination—to be for you a help and an invitation to faithfulness. I have written these words thinking of each one of you, and I embrace each one of you in my prayers.

Pupilla Oculi

I have also been thinking about the many young seminarians who are preparing for the priesthood. How often a Bishop turns his mind and heart to the seminary! It is the first object of his care and concern. We have a saying that *for a Bishop the seminary is the "apple of his eye."* A person protects his eyes because they enable him to see. In a way, the Bishop sees his Church through the seminary, since so much of ecclesial life depends on priestly vocations. The grace of numerous and holy vocations to the priesthood enables a Bishop to look with confidence to the future of his mission.

I say this on the basis of my many years of experience as a Bishop. I became a Bishop twelve years after my priestly ordination: a good part of these fifty years has been marked by this care for vocations. A Bishop's joy is great when the Lord gives vocations to his Church, while their absence causes him anxiety and concern. The Lord Jesus compared this concern to that of the reaper: "The harvest is plentiful, but the laborers are few; pray therefore the Lord of the harvest to send out laborers into his harvest" (Mt 9:37).

Deo Gratias!

I cannot end these reflections, in the year of my Golden Jubilee as a priest, without expressing to the Lord of the harvest my deepest gratitude for the gift of a vocation, for the grace of priesthood, for priestly vocations throughout the world. I do this in union with all the Bishops, who share the same concern for vocations and experience the same joy when their number increases. Thanks be to God, a certain crisis of priestly vocations in the Church is gradually being overcome. Each new priest brings with him a special blessing: "Blessed is he who comes in the name of the Lord." For in every priest it is Christ himself who comes. If, as Saint Cyprian said, the Christian is "another Christ"—*Christianus alter Christus*—with all the more reason it can be said: *Sacerdos alter Christus.*

May God sustain in all priests a grateful awareness of the gift they have received; may he also awaken in many young men a ready and generous response to his call to give themselves completely to the cause of the Gospel. The men and women of our time, who have such need of meaning and hope, will greatly benefit from their witness. And the Christian community will rejoice, knowing that it can look forward with confidence to the challenges of the approaching Third Millennium.

May the Virgin Mary accept this testimony of mine as a filial homage, for the glory of the Blessed Trinity. May she make it fruitful in the hearts of my brothers in the priesthood and of many members of the Church. May she make it a leaven of fraternity also for the many people who, although they do not share the same faith, often listen to my words and engage me in sincere dialogue.

LITANY OF
OUR LORD JESUS CHRIST,
PRIEST AND VICTIM

Kyrie eleison	*Kyrie, eleison*
Christe, eleison	*Christe, eleison*
Kyrie, eleison	*Kyrie, eleison*
Christe, audi nos	*Christe, audi nos*
Christe, exaudi nos	*Christe, exaudi nos*
Pater de caelis, Deus,	*miserere nobis*
Fili, Redemptor mundi, Deus,	*miserere nobis*
Spiritus Sancte, Deus,	*miserere nobis*
Sancta Trinitas, unus Deus,	*miserere nobis*
Iesu, Sacerdos et Victima,	*miserere nobis*
Iesu, Sacerdos in aeternum secundum ordinem Melchisedech,	*miserere nobis*
Iesu, Sacerdos quem misit Deus evangelizare pauperibus,	*miserere nobis*

Iesu, Sacerdos qui in novissima
   cena formam sacrificii perennis
   instituisti,   *miserere nobis*
Iesu, Sacerdos semper vivens ad
   interpellandum pro nobis,   *miserere nobis*
Iesu, Pontifex quem Pater unxit
   Spiritu Sancto et virtute,   *miserere nobis*
Iesu, Pontifex ex hominibus
   assumpte,   *miserere nobis*
Iesu, Pontifex pro hominibus
   constitute,   *miserere nobis*
Iesu, Pontifex confessionis
   nostrae,   *miserere nobis*
Iesu, Pontifex amplioris prae
   Moysi gloriae,   *miserere nobis*
Iesu, Pontifex tabernaculi veri,   *miserere nobis*
Iesu, Pontifex futurorum
   bonorum,   *miserere nobis*
Iesu, Pontifex sancte, innocens et
   impollute,   *miserere nobis*
Iesu, Pontifex fidelis et
   misericors,   *miserere nobis*
Iesu, Pontifex Dei et animarum
   zelo succense,   *miserere nobis*

Iesu, Pontifex in aeternum
    perfecte, *miserere nobis*

Iesu, Pontifex qui per proprium
    sanguinem caelos penetrasti, *miserere nobis*

Iesu, Pontifex qui nobis viam
    novam initiasti, *miserere nobis*

Iesu, Pontifex qui dilexisti nos et
    lavisti nos a peccatis in
    sanguine tuo, *miserere nobis*

Iesu, Pontifex qui tradidisti
    temetipsum Deo oblationem
    et hostiam, *miserere nobis*

Iesu, Hostia Dei et hominum, *miserere nobis*

Iesu, Hostia sancta et
    immaculata, *miserere nobis*

Iesu, Hostia placabilis, *miserere nobis*

Iesu, Hostia pacifica, *miserere nobis*

Iesu, Hostia propitiationis et
    laudis, *miserere nobis*

Iesu, Hostia reconciliationis et
    pacis, *miserere nobis*

Iesu, Hostia in qua habemus
    fiduciam et accessum ad
    Deum, *miserere nobis*

Iesu, Hostia vivens in saecula
   saeculorum,   *miserere nobis*

Propitius esto!   *parce nobis, Iesu*

Propitius esto!   *exaudi nos, Iesu*

A temerario in clerum ingressu,   *libera nos, Iesu*

A peccato sacrilegii,   *libera nos, Iesu*

A spiritu incontinentiae,   *libera nos, Iesu*

A turpi quaestu,   *libera nos, Iesu*

Ab omni simoniae labe,   *libera nos, Iesu*

Ab indigna opum
   ecclesiasticarum dispensatione, *libera nos, Iesu*

Ab amore mundi eiusque
   vanitatum,   *libera nos, Iesu*

Ab indigna Mysteriorum tuorum
   celebratione,   *libera nos, Iesu*

Per aeternum sacerdotium tuum, *libera nos, Iesu*

Per sanctam unctionem, qua a
   Deo Patre in sacerdotem
   constitutus es,   *libera nos, Iesu*

Per sacerdotalem spiritum tuum, *libera nos, Iesu*

Per ministerium illud, quo
   Patrem tuum super terram
   clarificasti,   *libera nos, Iesu*

Per cruentam tui ipsius

immolationem semel in cruce
factam,   *libera nos, Iesu*

Per illud idem sacrificium in
altari quotidie renovatum,   *libera nos, Iesu*

Per divinam illam potestatem,
quam in sacerdotibus tuis
invisibiliter exerces,   *libera nos, Iesu*

Ut universum ordinem
sacerdotalem in sancta
religione conservare digneris,   *Te rogamus, audi nos*

Ut pastores secundum cor tuum
populo tuo providere digneris,   *Te rogamus, audi nos*

Ut illos spiritus sacerdotii tui
implere digneris,   *Te rogamus, audi nos*

Ut labia sacerdotum scientiam
custodiant,   *Te rogamus, audi nos*

Ut in messem tuam operarios
fideles mittere digneris,   *Te rogamus, audi nos*

Ut fideles mysteriorum tuorum
dispensatores multiplicare
digneris,   *Te rogamus, audi nos*

Ut eis perseverantem in tua
voluntate famulatum tribuere
digneris,   *Te rogamus, audi nos*

Ut eis in ministerio
   mansuetudinem, in actione
   sollertiam et in oratione
   constantiam concedere
   digneris,   *Te rogamus, audi nos*
Ut per eos sanctissimi
   Sacramenti cultum ubique
   promovere digneris,   *Te rogamus, audi nos*
Ut qui tibi bene ministraverunt,
   in gaudium tuum suscipere
   digneris,   *Te rogamus, audi nos*
Agnus Dei, qui tollis peccata
   mundi,   *parce nobis, Domine*
Agnus Dei, qui tollis peccata
   mundi,   *exaudi nos, Domine*
Agnus Dei, qui tollis peccata
   mundi,   *miserere nobis, Domine*
Iesu, Sacerdos,   *audi nos*
Iesu, Sacerdos,   *exaudi nos*

OREMUS

   Ecclesiae tuae, Deus, sanctificator et custos, suscita in
ea per Spiritum tuum idoneos et fideles sanctorum

mysteriorum dispensatores, ut eorum ministerio et exemplo christiana plebs in viam salutis te protegente dirigatur. Per Christum Dominum nostrum. Amen.

Deus, qui ministrantibus et ieiunantibus discipulis segregari iussisti Saulum et Barnabam in opus ad quod assumpseras eos, adesto nunc Ecclesiae tuae oranti, et tu, qui omnium corda nosti, ostende quos elegeris in ministerium. Per Christum Dominum nostrum. Amen.

LITANY OF
OUR LORD JESUS CHRIST,
PRIEST AND VICTIM

Lord, have mercy	*Lord, have mercy*
Christ, have mercy	*Christ, have mercy*
Lord, have mercy	*Lord, have mercy*
Christ, hear us	*Christ, hear us*
Christ, heed our prayer	*Christ, heed our prayer*
Father in Heaven, God,	*have mercy on us*
Son, Redeemer of the world, God,	*have mercy on us*
Holy Spirit, God,	*have mercy on us*
Holy Trinity, one God,	*have mercy on us*
Jesus, Priest and Victim,	*have mercy on us*
Jesus, Priest forever, according to the order of Melchisedech,	*have mercy on us*
Jesus, Priest sent by God to preach the Gospel to the poor,	*have mercy on us*

Jesus, Priest who at the Last
Supper instituted the form of
the eternal sacrifice,   *have mercy on us*
Jesus, Priest living forever to
make intercession for us,   *have mercy on us*
Jesus, High Priest whom the
Father anointed with the Holy
Spirit and virtue,   *have mercy on us*
Jesus, High Priest taken up from
among men,   *have mercy on us*
Jesus, made High Priest for
men,   *have mercy on us*
Jesus, High Priest of our
confession of faith,   *have mercy on us*
Jesus, High Priest of greater
glory than Moses,   *have mercy on us*
Jesus, High Priest of the true
tabernacle,   *have mercy on us*
Jesus, High Priest of good things
to come,   *have mercy on us*
Jesus, holy High Priest, innocent
and undefiled,   *have mercy on us*
Jesus, faithful and merciful High
Priest,   *have mercy on us*

Jesus, High Priest of God, on
    fire with zeal for souls,   *have mercy on us*
Jesus, perfect High Priest forever,   *have mercy on us*
Jesus, High Priest who pierced
    heaven with your own blood,   *have mercy on us*
Jesus, High Priest who initiated
    us into a new life,   *have mercy on us*
Jesus, High Priest who loved us
    and washed us clean of our
    sins in your blood,   *have mercy on us*
Jesus, High Priest, who gave
    yourself up to God as offering
    and victim,   *have mercy on us*
Jesus, sacrificial victim of God
    and man,   *have mercy on us*
Jesus, holy and spotless sacrificial
    victim,   *have mercy on us*
Jesus, mild and gentle sacrificial
    victim,   *have mercy on us*
Jesus, peace-making sacrificial
    victim,   *have mercy on us*
Jesus, sacrificial victim of
    propitiation and praise,   *have mercy on us*

Jesus, sacrificial victim of reconciliation and peace,	*have mercy on us*
Jesus, sacrificial victim in whom we have confidence and access to God,	*have mercy on us*
Jesus, sacrificial victim living for ever and ever,	*have mercy on us*
Be gracious!	*spare us, Jesus*
Be gracious!	*hear us, Jesus*
From rashly entering the clergy,	*free us, Jesus*
From the sin of sacrilege,	*free us, Jesus*
From the spirit of incontinence,	*free us, Jesus*
From sordid self-interest	*free us, Jesus*
From every lapse into simony,	*free us, Jesus*
From the unworthy administration of the Church's treasures,	*free us, Jesus*
From the love of the world and its vanities,	*free us, Jesus*
From the unworthy celebration of your Mysteries,	*free us, Jesus*
Through your eternal priesthood,	*free us, Jesus*
Through the holy anointing by	

which God the Father made
you a priest,   *free us, Jesus*
Through your priestly spirit,   *free us, Jesus*
Through the ministry by which
you glorified your Father on
this earth,   *free us, Jesus*
Through the bloody immolation
of yourself made once and for
all on the cross,   *free us, Jesus*
Through that same sacrifice,
daily renewed on the altar,   *free us, Jesus*
Through the divine power that
you exercise invisibly in your
priests,   *free us, Jesus*
That you may kindly maintain
the whole priestly order in
holy religion,   *hear us, we beseech You*
That you may kindly provide
your people with pastors after
your own heart,   *hear us, we beseech You*
That you may kindly fill them
with the spirit of your
priesthood,   *hear us, we beseech You*
That the lips of your priests

may be repositories of
knowledge,   *hear us, we beseech You*

That you may kindly send
faithful workers into your
harvest,   *hear us, we beseech You*

That you may kindly increase
the faithful dispensers of your
mysteries,   *hear us, we beseech You*

That you may kindly grant them
persevering obedience to your
will,   *hear us, we beseech You*

That you may kindly give them
gentleness in their ministry,
skill in their actions, and
constancy in their prayer,   *hear us, we beseech You*

That through them you may
kindly promote the veneration
of the Blessed Sacrament all
over the world,   *hear us, we beseech You*

That you may kindly receive into
your joy those who have
served you well,   *hear us, we beseech You*

Lamb of God, who take away
the sins of the world,   *spare us, o Lord*

Lamb of God, who take away
    the sins of the world, *hear us, o Lord*
Lamb of God, who take away
    the sins of the world, *have mercy on us, o Lord*
Jesus, our Priest, *hear us*
Jesus, our Priest, *heed our prayers*

LET US PRAY

O God, sanctifier and guardian of your Church, stir up in her through your Spirit suitable and faithful dispensers of the holy mysteries, so that by their ministry and example the Christian people may be guided in the path of salvation with your protection. Through Christ, our Lord. Amen.

God, who, when the disciples ministered to the Lord and fasted, ordered that Saul and Barnabas be set aside for the work to which you called them, be with your Church as she prays now, and you, who know the hearts of all of us, show those whom you have chosen for your ministry. Through Christ, our Lord. Amen.